Rally Car Race

Story by Annette Smith
Illustrations by Richard Hoit

Zac loved watching rally cars on TV.

One day,
a man came to live next door
to Zac's family.
He owned a real rally car.
It was bright red and yellow,
and it had special tyres.
The man locked it in his garage
where it was safe.

Every weekend,
the man would bring the rally car
out of the garage.
Zac often stood at the fence
and watched.

The man would walk around his car
and clean it.
He would look underneath it
and check the engine.

One Saturday, Zac called out,
"Please can I come
and look at your car?"

"No, I'm too busy,"
said the man, sounding annoyed.
"This car is going
in an important race next weekend."

"Don't worry, Zac," said his father.
"I know where that race will be held.
I'll take you to see it."

The next Saturday, Zac and his dad stood with the other people at the sideline.

They watched the teams getting the rally cars ready for the races.

"There's the man from next door!" shouted Zac.
"Hello! Hello!" he called to him.

The man nodded at Zac, and turned away quickly.

The cars in the first race
sped off up the winding road.

Then, to Zac's surprise,
the man from next door
came running over to them.

"I've forgotten my special helmet,"
he said. "It's in the garage at home.
I can't race my car without it.
Could you go back and get it for me
in time for the third race, please?"

"Yes," said Zac's dad.
"We'll get your helmet for you."

"Thank you!" said the man.
"Here are the keys to the garage."

Soon Zac and his dad were back with the man's special helmet.

The man was smiling now.
"Thanks," he said, putting it on.
"My race is about to start.
I hope you will come back and see me when all the races are finished."

3
1
1

Zac and his dad watched the man drive his car up the winding road and over the hill.
The car was going very fast!

They waited and waited for a long time.
Then they saw a cloud of dust in the distance.

"Wow! Look!" shouted Zac.
"The car from next door is in the lead! It's going to win!"

CONTROL

After the races had finished, the man from next door came over to Zac and Dad.

"My name's Mark," he said to them. "Come and see my car. Thanks to you, I won my race."

Zac walked around the car. Then Mark winked at Zac and handed him a helmet.

"I need a new co-driver," he said. "Let's go for a little ride."

CON
1
1

Zac clipped on his seat belt
and away they went
around a part of the track,
and back to Dad.

"That was great!" said Zac.

"Yes," laughed Mark,
"and please come over and help me
with my car next weekend."